ISBN: 978-1-6289-0653-0

First Edition: Rabee' Thani 1435 A.H. / March 2014 C.E.

Cover Design: Aboo Sulaymaan Muhammad 'Abdul-Azim bin Joshua Baker
E-mail: info@maktabatulirshad.com

Translation by: Aboo Sulaymaan Muhammad 'Abdul-Azim bin Joshua Baker

Revision of Translation by: Aboo Ruqayyah Raha Ibn Donald Batts

Editing by: Deliberate Ink
E-mail: shakirah@deliberateink.com

Typesetting and Formatting: Aboo Sulaymaan Muhammad 'Abdul-Azim bin Joshua Baker

Printing: Ohio Printing

Subject: Hadeeth

Website: www.maktabatulirshad.com
E-mail: info@maktabatulirshad.com

TABLE OF CONTENTS

BIOGRAPHY OF THE EXPLAINER

Al-Allaamah Muhammad Bin Saleh Al-'Uthaymeen (1347-1421AH)

His lineage and birth: He is the noble scholar, verifier, Faqeeh, scholar of Tafsir, god-fearing, ascetic, Muhammad Bin Saleh Bin Muhammad bin Sulaymaan bin 'Abd-Rahman Ali 'Uthaymeen from *Al-Wahbah* of Bani Tameem. He was born on the 27th night of the blessed month Ramadan in the year 1347AH in 'Unayzah –one of the cities of Al-Qaseem- in the kingdom of Saudia Arabia.

His scholastic upbringing: his father, may Allaah have mercy upon him, enrolled him to study the Noble Quran with his maternal grandfather, the teacher 'Abdur-Rahman Bin Sulaymaan Ad-Daamigh', may Allaah have mercy upon him. Then he studied writing, some arithmetic, and Arabic literature at *"Al-Ustaadh 'Abdul-Azeez Bin Saleh Ad-Daamigh's school"*; and that was before he enrolled in *"Al-Mu'allim*

'Ali Bin 'Abdillah Ash-Shahaytan's School" where he memorized the Noble Quran with him, and he had not reached fourteen years of age yet.

Under the direction of his father, may Allaah have mercy upon him, he embarked upon seeking religious knowledge; and the noble Shaykh Al-'Allamah 'Abdur Rahman Bin Nasir As-Sa'dee, may Allâh have mercy upon him, use to teach religious sciences and Arabic at "*Jaame' Kabeer*" (i.e. Grand masjid where Jumu'ah his held) in 'Unayzah. He arranged two of his senior students to teach the beginning students. Therefore, the Shaykh (i.e. Al-'Uthaymeen) would join Shaykh Muhammad Bin 'Abdul-'Azeez Al-Mutawwa's circle of knowledge, may Allâh have mercy upon him, until he attained from knowledge of *Tawheed, Fiqh,* and *Nahw* (i.e. Arabic grammar related to the ending of words) what he attained.

Then he sat in the circles of knowledge of his Shaykh 'Abdur Rahman Bin Nasir As-Sa'dee, may Allaah have mercy upon him. So he studied with him Tafsir, Hadith, Seerah of the Prophet, At-Tawheed, Al-Fiqh, Al-'Usool, Al-Faraa'id, An-

Nahw, and memorization concise texts on these sciences.

The noble Shaykh Al-'Allamah 'Abdur Rahman Bin Nasir As-Sa'dee, May Allaah have mercy upon him, was considered to be his first Shaykh. Since he acquired knowledge, experience, and methods (of learning) from him more so than anyone else; and he was impressed by his methodology, his principles, his way of teaching, and his adherence to proofs and evidences.

When Shaykh 'Abdur-Rahman Bin 'Ali Bin 'Awdaan, may Allaah have mercy upon him, was a judge in 'Unayzah he (i.e. Shaykh Al-'Uthaymeen) would study the science of Al-Faraa'id with him, just like he would study An-Nahw and Al-Balaghah with Shaykh 'Abdur-Razzaaq 'Afeefee, may Allâh have mercy upon him, during his presence as a teacher in that city.

When the academic institution opened in Riyadh, some of his brothers urged him to enroll. So he sought his Shaykh's, 'Abdur Rahman Bin Nasir As-Sa'dee, may Allaah have mercy upon him, permission. So he gave him permission, and he enrolled in the institution from 1372AH to 1373AH.

Indeed he took advantage of the scholars who use to teach there at that time, through the two years that he entered in the academic institution in Riyadh. Among them was Al-'Allamah, scholar in Tafsir Shaykh Muhammad Al-Ameen As-Shanqitee, Shaykh Al-Faqeeh 'Abdul-'Azeez Bin Nasir Bin Rasheed, and Shaykh, the scholar in hadith, 'Abdur-Rahman Al-Ifreekee...may Allaah have mercy upon them.

During that time, he would stick with His eminence Shaykh Al-'Allamah 'Abdul-'Azeez Bin 'Abdillah Bin Baaz, may Allaah have mercy upon him, and he studied with him Saheeh Bukhari and some treatises of Shaykhul-Islam Ibn Taymiyah in the masjid. He benefited by him in the science of hadith, analyzing the views of the scholars of fiqh and the relationship between them. He considered Shaykh 'Abdul-'Azeez Bin Baaz, may Allaah have mercy upon him, to be his second Shaykh in obtaining knowledge and being influenced by him.

Then he returned to 'Unayzah in 1374AH, and he commenced studying under his Shaykh Al-'Allamah 'Abdur-Rahman Bin Nasir As-Sa'dee and he followed up his studies in the faculty of Sharee'ah, which had become a subsidiary of Imam Muhammad Bin Saud Islamic University until he obtained a high-ranking degree.

His teaching: his Shaykh saw in him nobleness and quickness in the acquisition of knowledge, so he encouraged him to teach while he was still a student in his circles of knowledge. So he began teaching in 1370 at the "*Jaamee Kabeer*" in 'Unayzah.

When he graduated from the institute in Riyadh, he was appointed as a teacher at the institution in 'Unayzah in 1374AH.

In 1376AH, his Shaykh Al-'Allamah 'Abdur-Rahman Bin Nasir as-Sa'dee, may Allaah have mercy upon him, died. Therefore, he (i.e. Al-'Uthaymeen) was appointed the imamate of "Jaamee Kabeer" in 'Unayzah and also he was appointed the imamate of two 'Eid there, and he was appointed to teach in the library of 'Unayzah Al-Wataniyah next to Jaamee Kabeer, which his Shaykh, founded in 1359AH.

When the number of students increased, and the library could not suffice them, the noble Shaykh began teaching in the Masjid Al-Jaamee. The students gathered there, and they would flock together from Kingdom of Saudia Arabia and outside of the Kingdom until they reached in the hundreds for some of the classes. These people studied seriously, and they did not just simply listened to the classes. He (i.e. 'Uthaymeen) remained upon that as an Imam, a Khateeb, and a teacher until his passing, may Allaah have mercy upon him.

The Shaykh remained a teacher in the institution from 1374AH to 1398AH, and when he transferred to teaching in the faculty of *Sharee'ah* and *Usool-Deen* in Al-Qaseem branch to Muhammad Bin Saud Islamic University and remained as a teacher there until his passing away, May Allaah the most high have mercy upon him.

He use to lecture in *Masjid Haram* and *Masjid An-Nabawi* during the seasons of Hajj, Ramadan, and the summer vacations from 1402AH until his passing away, may Allaah have mercy upon him.

The Shaykh had a particular teaching practice in his openhandedness and integrity. He would raise questions to his students, receive their questions, and hold classes and lectures with a lofty concern, a composed mind and delighted at his propagating religious knowledge and his closeness to the people.

His passing away: He passed away, may Allaah have mercy upon him, in the city of Jeddah shortly before Maghrib on Wednesday the 15th of the month of Shawwal 1421AH. He was prayed over in *Masjid Haram* after 'Asr on Thursday. Then he was followed by thousands who had prayed over him, and he was buried in *Mecca Al-Mukaramah.* [1]

[1] The source of this is biography was from the Shaykh's website (www.ibnothaimeen.com)

CHAPTER 71

HUMILITY AND LOWERING ONE'S WING TO THE BELIEVERS

Allaah the Sublime says,

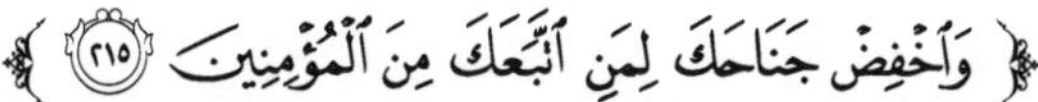

"And be kind and humble to the believers who follow you." [2]

And Allaah the Sublime says,

﴿ يَٰٓأَيُّهَا ٱلَّذِينَ ءَامَنُواْ مَن يَرْتَدَّ مِنكُمْ عَن دِينِهِۦ فَسَوْفَ يَأْتِى ٱللَّهُ بِقَوْمٍ يُحِبُّهُمْ
وَيُحِبُّونَهُۥٓ أَذِلَّةٍ عَلَى ٱلْمُؤْمِنِينَ أَعِزَّةٍ عَلَى ٱلْكَٰفِرِينَ ﴾

"O you who believe! Whoever from among you turns back from his religion (Islâm), Allaah will bring a people whom He will love and they will love Him;

[2] Ash-Shu'araa (26:215)

humble towards the believers, stern towards the disbelievers." [3]

And Allaah the Sublime says,

﴿ يَـٰٓأَيُّهَا ٱلنَّاسُ إِنَّا خَلَقْنَـٰكُم مِّن ذَكَرٍ وَأُنثَىٰ وَجَعَلْنَـٰكُمْ شُعُوبًا وَقَبَآئِلَ لِتَعَارَفُوٓا۟ ۚ إِنَّ أَكْرَمَكُمْ عِندَ ٱللَّهِ أَتْقَىٰكُمْ ﴾

"O mankind! We have created you from a male and a female, and made you into nations and tribes, that you may know one another. Verily, the most honorable of you with Allaah is that (believer) who has *At-Taqwaa*." [4]

And Allaah the Sublime says,

﴿ فَلَا تُزَكُّوٓا۟ أَنفُسَكُمْ ۖ هُوَ أَعْلَمُ بِمَنِ ٱتَّقَىٰٓ ﴿٣٢﴾ ﴾

"So ascribe not purity to yourselves. He knows best him who fears Allaah and keeps his duty to Him." [5]

And Allaah the Sublime says,

---

[3] Al-Māidah (5:54)
[4] Al-Hujuraat (49:13)
[5] An-Najm (53:32)

﴿ وَنَادَىٰٓ أَصْحَـٰبُ ٱلْأَعْرَافِ رِجَالًا يَعْرِفُونَهُم بِسِيمَـٰهُمْ قَالُوا۟ مَآ أَغْنَىٰ عَنكُمْ جَمْعُكُمْ وَمَا كُنتُمْ تَسْتَكْبِرُونَ ﴿٤٨﴾ أَهَـٰٓؤُلَآءِ ٱلَّذِينَ أَقْسَمْتُمْ لَا يَنَالُهُمُ ٱللَّهُ بِرَحْمَةٍ ۚ ٱدْخُلُوا۟ ٱلْجَنَّةَ لَا خَوْفٌ عَلَيْكُمْ وَلَآ أَنتُمْ تَحْزَنُونَ ﴿٤٩﴾ ﴾

"And the men on *Al-A'râf* (the wall) will call unto the men whom they would recognize by their marks, saying: "Of what benefit to you were your great numbers (and hoards of wealth), and your arrogance against Faith?" Are they those about whom you swore that Allaah would never show them mercy? (Behold! It has been said to them): 'Enter Paradise, no fear shall be on you, nor shall you grieve.'" [6]

Explanation

An-Nawawi *(rahimahullah)* said in the book *Riyadh As-Saaliheen,* in the chapter "Humility and lowering one's wing to the believers":

[6] Al-A'raaf (7:48-49)

HUMILITY AND LOWERING ONE'S WING TO THE BELIEVERS

Humility is the opposite of self-exaltation. Humility is that one does not elevate or exalt himself over others by way of his knowledge, lineage, wealth, status, leadership, governorship, and so on. Rather, it is obligatory to lower one's wing to the believers. He should exhibit kindness to them just as the most honorable of creation and lofty amongst them before Allaah, the Messenger of Allaah *(sallallahu alayhi wa sallam),* used to exhibit kindness to the believers, to the point that a young girl would grab him by the hand and take him wherever she wanted and he would fulfill her need for her.

Allaah the Sublime says,

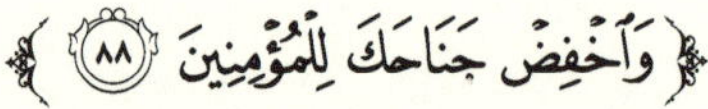

> **"And be kind and humble to the believers."** [7]

And in another verse Allaah says,

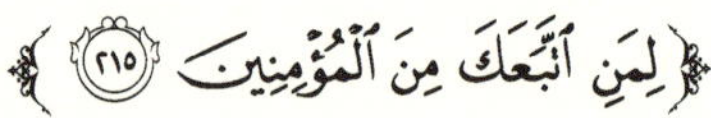

"the believers who follow you." [8]

---

[7] Al-Hijr (15:88)
[8] Ash-Shuraa' (26:215)

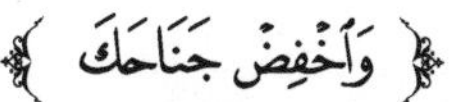

"... and lower your wing"

Meaning be humble. The arrogant and haughty person thinks of himself as a bird soaring in the air. So he is commanded to lower his wing and come down to the believers who follow the Prophet *(sallallahu alayhi wa sallam).*

It is known that one is not to lower one's wing to the disbeliever. Rather, one is to be elevated above the disbeliever and exalted above him, placing himself in a position above him. Cling to the Statement of Allaah (*At-Tawheed*), and the Statement of Allaah is superior. Allaah said in his description of the Prophet *(sallallahu alayhi wa sallam)* and his companions,

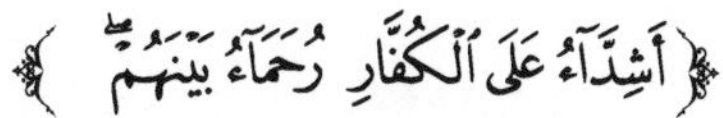

"They are severe against disbelievers, and merciful among themselves," [9]

Meaning they are stern and firm against the disbelievers while compassionate to each other.

[9] Al-Fath (48:29)

Then, the mentioned the second verse, Allaah the Sublime's statement,

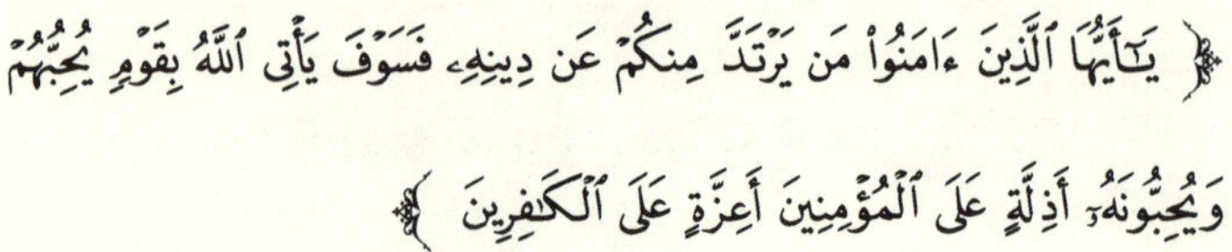

> **"O you who believe! Whoever from among you turns back from his religion (Islâm), Allaah will bring a people whom He will love and they will love Him; humble towards the believers, stern towards the disbelievers."** [10]

Perhaps a person enters Islam and acts according to it, and afterward Shaytaan misguides him—and the refuge is with Allaah—until he apostates from the religion. When he apostates, he is no longer an ally or supporter of the believers. Because of this, Allaah says,

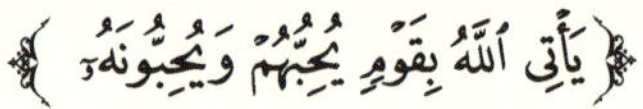

> **"Allaah will bring a people whom He will love and they will love Him,"**

meaning, a believing people.

---

[10] Al-Māidah (5:54)

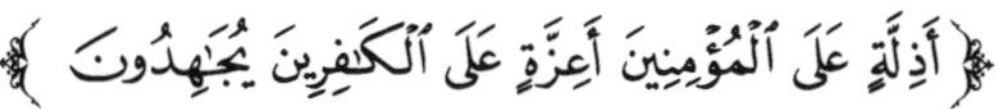

"... humble towards the believers, stern towards the disbelievers."

They are to the believers humble, not raising their status above them or asserting their might over them. Toward the disbelievers, they are dignified in their status. The Prophet (*sallallahu 'alayhi wa sallam*) said,

لَا تَبْدَؤُوا الْيَهُودَ وَ النَّصَارَى بِالسَّلَامِ ، وَ إِذَا لَقِيتُمُوهُم فِي طَرِيقٍ فَاضْطَرُّوهُمْ إِلَى أضيقِهِ

"do not initiate the greetings to the Jews and Christians; when you meet them in the road force them to its edges." [11]

This is to subdue them and forsake them. They are your Lord's enemy, your messenger's enemy, the enemies of your religion, and the enemies of the book of Allaah.

---

[11] Muslim collected it in Kitaabul Salaam under the chapter "The prohibition of initiating the greetings to the people of the book" (2166)

Within this verse is evidence for the affirmation of love from Allaah the Mighty and Majestic, and that Allaah loves and is loved.

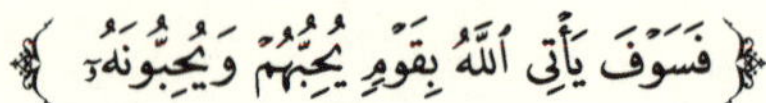

"Allaah will bring a people whom He will love and they will love Him."

This love is tremendous, and has no equivalent. You find that for the one who loves Allaah, the Mighty and Majestic, the *Dunya,* family, and wealth are of little value to him. Even his own self (is of little value to him) compared to that which is pleasing to Allaah, the Mighty and Majestic.

Because of this, one sacrifices and exposes his neck to Allaah's enemies, out of love for giving victory to Allaah, the Mighty and Majestic and giving victory to His religion. And this is evidence that one must give precedence to that which Allaah and His Messenger love over that which one loves oneself.

From the signs that one loves Allaah is that one is constant in the remembrance of Allaah. He remembers his Lord constantly within his heart, tongue, and limbs.

Another sign that one loves Allaah is that one loves whomever Allaah loves. So He loves the messenger (*sallallahu 'alayhi wa sallam*), the rightly guided successors, the Imams, and whomever is in his time from the people of knowledge and righteousness.

Yet another sign that one loves Allaah is that one establishes obedience to Allaah and places it before one's desires. When the caller to prayer calls out, "Come to the prayer," one leaves one's work and comes to the prayer because one loves that which pleases Allaah more than that which is pleasing to his soul.

Allaah's love has many signs. When one loves his Lord, Allaah the Mighty and Sublime hastens to love him, as Allaah, the Glorified and Sublime says in the *qudsi* hadith,

وَ مَنْ أَتَانِي يَمْشِي أَتَيْتُهُ هَرْوَلَةً.

"The one who comes to Me walking I will come to him at a quick pace." [12]

---

[12] Al-Bukhari collected it in Kitaabul Tawheed under the chapter "Allaah, the Sublime's statement, 'Allaah warns you of himself'" (7405); and Muslim collected it in Kitaabul

Because of this Allaah the Sublime says,

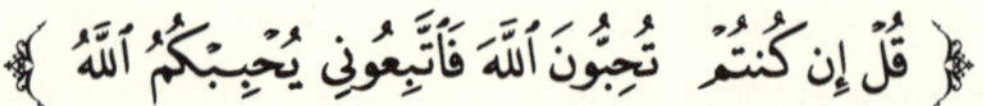

> **"Say (O Muhammad to mankind): "If you (really) love Allaah then follow me (i.e. accept Islâmic Monotheism, follow the Qur'ân and the *Sunnah*), Allaah will love you."** [13]

Allaah did not order the Prophet (*sallallahu 'alayhi wa sallam*) to say, "Follow me (Muhammad) and believe in Allaah." Rather He says, "Allaah will love you." For this is the fruit: Allaah will love His servant. When He loves His servant, the servant has attained the good of the *Dunya* and the Hereafter. May Allaah make me and you among His beloved.

Within Allaah's statement **"they love Him"** is evidence for the affirmation of the servant's love for His Lord; and this is something witnessed. One finds within one's heart a fervent desire for whatever pleases Allaah. This shows that Allaah the Mighty and Sublime loves him.

Dhikr and Du'aa under the chapter "Encouragement to remember Allaah the Sublime." (2675)

[13] Ali Imraan (3:31)

The believing person who has been granted success (by Allaah) with this great characteristic is one who loves Allaah more than oneself, children, mother and father, or anything else. He is one who loves another person because that other person loves Allaah, as it is well-known that one is fond of those beloved to one's beloved. Thus due to one's love for Allaah, one loves those whom Allaah the Mighty and Sublime loves of people, actions, and statements.

Then the author, Al-Haafidh An-Nawawi, may Allaah have mercy upon him, mentioned in his book *Riyaadh As-Saaliheen* under the heading: "The chapter of humility and lowering one's wing to the believers"—after citing the verse:

﴿ يَـٰٓأَيُّهَا ٱلنَّاسُ إِنَّا خَلَقْنَـٰكُم مِّن ذَكَرٍ وَأُنثَىٰ وَجَعَلْنَـٰكُمْ شُعُوبًا وَقَبَآئِلَ لِتَعَارَفُوٓا۟ ۚ إِنَّ أَكْرَمَكُمْ عِندَ ٱللَّهِ أَتْقَىٰكُمْ ۚ إِنَّ ٱللَّهَ عَلِيمٌ خَبِيرٌ ﴿١٣﴾ ﴾

"O mankind! We have created you from a male and a female, and made you into nations and tribes, that you may know one another. Verily, the most honorable of you with Allaah is that (believer) who has *At-Taqwa* [i.e. one of the *Muttaqûn*.

Verily, Allaah is All-Knowing, All-Aware." [14]

Allaah, the Mighty and Sublime, addresses all of mankind, declaring that He created them from a male and female. "Male and female" refers to Aadam and Hawaa' or simply means that all the children of Aadam were created from a male and a female. The latter is the predominant view and the most commonly used.

Allaah created Aadam without a mother and father, from dirt, mud, then dry clay. Then He created for him a soul and blew it into him, so he became a well-proportioned human being. Allaah created Hawaa' from a father without a mother. Allaah created 'Esaa from a mother without a father. Allaah created the rest of humanity from a mother and a father.

Just as the human being is of four types as it relates to the basis of his creation, he is of four types as it relates to the gender of that which is created (i.e., his offspring). Allaah the Mighty and Sublime says,

[14] Al-Hujuraat (49:13)

﴿ لِّلَّهِ مُلْكُ ٱلسَّمَٰوَٰتِ وَٱلْأَرْضِ ۚ يَخْلُقُ مَا يَشَآءُ ۚ يَهَبُ لِمَن يَشَآءُ إِنَٰثًا وَيَهَبُ لِمَن يَشَآءُ ٱلذُّكُورَ ﴿٤٩﴾ أَوْ يُزَوِّجُهُمْ ذُكْرَانًا وَإِنَٰثًا ۖ وَيَجْعَلُ مَن يَشَآءُ عَقِيمًا ۚ إِنَّهُۥ عَلِيمٌ قَدِيرٌ ﴿٥٠﴾ ﴾

"To Allaah belongs the kingdom of the heavens and the earth. He creates what He wills. He bestows female (offspring) upon whom He wills, and bestows male (offspring) upon whom He wills. Or He bestows both males and females, and He renders barren whom He wills. Verily, He is the All-Knower and is Able to do all things." [15]

"He bestows female (offspring) upon whom He wills," meaning no male (offspring). Some people have daughters and no sons.

"and bestows male (offspring) upon whom He wills." meaning male offspring only.

"Or He bestows both males and females." The (Arabic word for) "mate" can refer to "kind" as well, just as Allaah the Sublime says,

---

[15] Ash-Shuraa' (42:49-50)

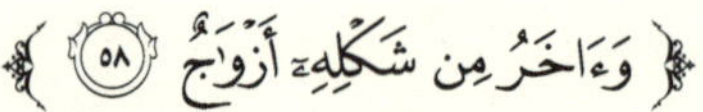

"And other torments of similar kinds, all together!" [16]

meaning in pairs.

And Allaah says,

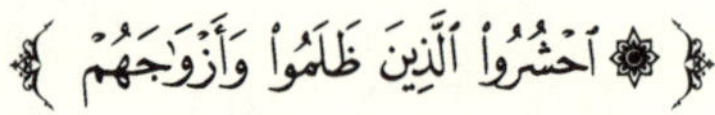

"(It will be said to the angels): "Assemble those who did wrong, together with their companions (from the devils)," [17]

Meaning, their types. Thus He pairs the two types together, male and female offspring.

The fourth category, **"and He renders barren whom He wills."** Some do not have any sons or daughters. Allaah the Glorified and Sublime owns the dominion of the heavens and earth; He creates whatever He wills. No one can amend His ruling and He is All-Seeing and All-Knowing.

---

[16] Saad (38:58)
[17] Saffaat (37:22)

Allaah, Great is His Mention, says, **"and made you into nations and tribes."** The word "nations" refers to large groups of people, just as "the Arab" refers to all kinds of Arabs; and "the non-Arab" refers to all other races. Tribes are smaller groups of people. The Quraysh, Banu Tameem, and so forth (within the Arab nation) are tribes.

Allaah's statement, **"that you may know one another."** This (statement) is the wisdom behind Allaah making us into nations and tribes. Allaah made these tribes for the purpose of us knowing one another, not for the purpose of boasting to one another saying, "I am Arab and you are non-Arab; I belong to a tribe and you are *khudhairi* [18]; I am wealthy and you are poor." These are phrases from the pre-Islamic period, and the refuge is with Allaah. The Prophet (*'alayhi salaatu wa sallam*) said,

---

[18] Translator's note: A common word used especially among the people of Najd and Saudi Arabia in general to describe those whose Arab origin is unknown.

إِنَّ اللهَ أَذْهَبَ عَنْكُمْ عُبِيَّةَ الْجَاهِلِيَّةِ وَ فَخْرَهَا بِالْآبَاءِ، مُؤْمِنٌ تَقِيٌّ وَ فَاجِرٌ شَقِيٌّ، أَنْتُمْ بَنُو آدَامَ وَ آدَامُ مِنْ تُرَابٍ.

"Indeed Allaah has removed the haughtiness of the pre-Islamic period, and the boasting of one's forefathers. One is either a pious believer or a wicked evil-doer. You all are the children of Aadam and he is from dirt." [19]

The most noble among us before Allaah is he who has the most *taqwaa* of Allaah the Mighty and Sublime. Nonetheless, it is imperative we know that some tribes or some nations are more virtuous than others. The nation to which the Messenger (*'alayhi wa salaatu wa sallam*) was sent is the most virtuous. The nation of Arabs is more virtuous than the rest as Allaah says in his book,

---

19 Aboo Dawud collected it in *Kitaabul-Adab* under the chapter "Mutually boasting of nobility" (5116); and At-Tirmidhi collected it in *Kitaabul-Munaqib* under the chapter "Regarding the excellence of Sham and Yemen." (3956)

﴿ ٱللَّهُ أَعْلَمُ حَيْثُ يَجْعَلُ رِسَالَتَهُۥ ﴾

"Allaah knows best with whom to place His Message." [20]

The Prophet (*sallallahu 'alayhi wa sallam*) said,

النَّاسُ مَعَادِنٌ خِيَارُهُمْ فِي الْجَاهِلِيَّةِ خِيَارُهُمْ فِي الإِسْلَامِ إِذَا فَقَهُوا.

"People are of different natures. The best of them during the pre-Islamic period of ignorance are the best of them in Al-Islaam if they acquire understanding of the religion."[21]

This does not denote disdain for the rest of human race; boasting is not allowed. As for variation in virtue, Allaah gives preferences to some races over others. The Arab is more virtuous than the non-Arab; nevertheless, if the

---

[20] Al-An'aam (6:124)

[21] Al-Bukhari collected it in *Kitaabul-Munaqib* under the chapter "Allaah the Sublime's statement, 'O mankind, we created you...'" (3493); and Muslim collected it in *Kitaabul Fadaa'il Sahaabah* under the chapter "The best of mankind." (2526)

Arab is impious and the non-Arab has *taqwaa* then the non-Arab is more noble before Allaah than the Arab.

Afterward, the author quotes:

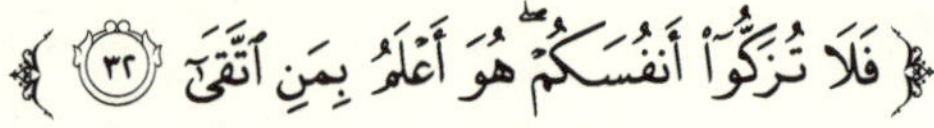

> **"So ascribe not purity to yourselves. He knows best him who fears and keeps his duty to Him [i.e. those who are *Al-Muttaqûn*]."** [22]

"So ascribe not purity" means to not commend oneself in claiming righteousness. However, speaking about Allaah's blessing upon a servant like mentioning how one used to transgress bounds and was deviated (from guidance) so Allaah guided and granted one *tawfeeq,* and how he gained uprightness in the religion—this is speaking about the favor of Allaah, and not purifying oneself. There is no harm in this, just as there is no harm in mentioning the favor of Allah's enriching one after poverty.

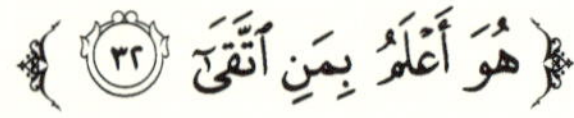

---

22 An-Najm (53:32)

"He knows best him who fears and keep his duty to Him."

The word "He" is referring the Lord, the Mighty and Majestic. How often do two individuals seek knowledge or claim to implement it, yet the difference between them in *taqwaa* is like the distance between the heavens and earth. Two people praying next to one another may have in their hearts of *taqwaa* a difference similar to the distance between the heavens and earth. This is why Allaah says,

﴿فَلَا تُزَكُّوٓا۟ أَنفُسَكُمْ ۖ هُوَ أَعْلَمُ بِمَنِ ٱتَّقَىٰٓ ﴿٣٢﴾﴾

"So ascribe not purity to yourselves. He knows best him who fears and keep his duty to Him [i.e. those who are *Al-Muttaqûn*]."

Afterward the author cites another verse, which is the statement of Allaah the Sublime,

﴿وَنَادَىٰٓ أَصْحَـٰبُ ٱلْأَعْرَافِ رِجَالًا يَعْرِفُونَهُم بِسِيمَـٰهُمْ قَالُوا۟ مَآ أَغْنَىٰ عَنكُمْ جَمْعُكُمْ وَمَا كُنتُمْ تَسْتَكْبِرُونَ ﴿٤٨﴾﴾

"And the men on *Al-A'râf* (the wall) will call unto the men whom they would

> **recognize by their marks, saying: 'Of what benefit to you were your great numbers (and hoards of wealth), and your arrogance against Faith?'"** [23]

The companions of *Al-A'raf* are people whose good and bad deeds are equal. They don't enter Paradise or Hell. The inhabitants of Hell are gathered into Hell and the inhabitants of paradise taken as delegates to meet Ar-Rahmaan, in groups. Yet the companions of *Al-A'raf*. The word *Al-A'raf* is the plural of *'Arf*, which is an elevated place; however, they are neither in Paradise nor the Fire. They (the companions of *Al-A'raf*) will observe both inhabitants and eventually they will enter Paradise since eventually no places will remain except Paradise and Hell.

Allaah the Sublime says,

﴿ وَنَادَىٰٓ أَصۡحَٰبُ ٱلۡأَعۡرَافِ رِجَالٗا يَعۡرِفُونَهُم بِسِيمَىٰهُمۡ ﴾

> **"And the men on *Al-A'râf* (the wall) will call unto the men whom they would recognize by their marks."**

[23] Al-'Araaf (7:48)

They will completely recognize them by their signs.

﴿قَالُوا۟ مَآ أَغْنَىٰ عَنكُمْ جَمْعُكُمْ وَمَا كُنتُمْ تَسْتَكْبِرُونَ ﴿٤٨﴾﴾

"... saying: 'Of what benefit to you were your great numbers (and hoards of wealth), and your arrogance against Faith?'"

meaning, your wealth, children, and family did not avail you; your armies, did not avail you; gathering them and seeking their assistance did not avail you in the least.

﴿وَمَا كُنتُمْ تَسْتَكْبِرُونَ ﴿٤٨﴾﴾

"...and your arrogance against Faith?"

meaning, your arrogance against the truth, did it avail you?

﴿أَهَـٰٓؤُلَآءِ ٱلَّذِينَ أَقْسَمْتُمْ لَا يَنَالُهُمُ ٱللَّهُ بِرَحْمَةٍ﴾

"Are they those, of whom you swore that Allaah would never show them mercy?"

Meaning, the weak. The leaders rejected the messengers, mocked the believers, and said,

﴿ أَهَٰٓؤُلَآءِ مَنَّ ٱللَّهُ عَلَيۡهِم مِّنۢ بَيۡنِنَآ ﴾

"Is it these (poor believers) that Allaah has favored from amongst us?" [24]

The people of *Al-A'raf* will say, "Aren't they the people who have mercy upon them—the inhabitants of Paradise whom you mocked (as being weak)?"

﴿ إِنَّ ٱلَّذِينَ أَجۡرَمُواْ كَانُواْ مِنَ ٱلَّذِينَ ءَامَنُواْ يَضۡحَكُونَ ﴿٢٩﴾ وَإِذَا مَرُّواْ
بِهِمۡ يَتَغَامَزُونَ ﴿٣٠﴾ وَإِذَا ٱنقَلَبُوٓاْ إِلَىٰٓ أَهۡلِهِمُ ٱنقَلَبُواْ فَكِهِينَ ﴿٣١﴾ ﴾

"Verily! (During the worldly life) those who committed crimes used to laugh at those who believed. And whenever they passed by them, used to wink one to another (in mockery). And when they returned to their own people, they would return jesting." [25]

So they will say to them (i.e., the weak),

﴿ أَهَٰٓؤُلَآءِ ٱلَّذِينَ أَقۡسَمۡتُمۡ لَا يَنَالُهُمُ ٱللَّهُ بِرَحۡمَةٍۚ ٱدۡخُلُواْ ٱلۡجَنَّةَ ﴾

---

24 Al-'An'aam (6:53)
25 Al-Mutaffifin (83:29-31)

"Is it these (poor believers) that Allaah has favored from amongst us?"

It will be said to them (i.e., the weak),

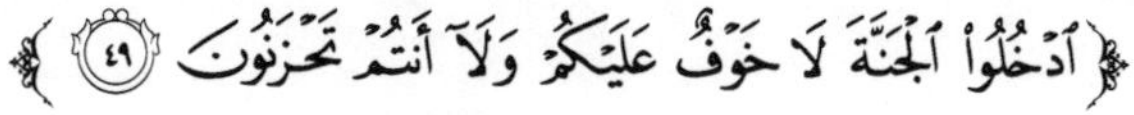

"Enter Paradise. No fear shall be on you, nor shall you grieve."

Their humility toward the truth and their following the Messengers helped them attain these lofty stations. As for those arrogant individuals who boasted about what Allaah granted them of large armies and wealth, indeed that will not avail them in the least. So this proves the virtue of humbling oneself to the truth.

We ask Allaah to make us and you among those who are humble to Him and towards the truth the messengers brought; indeed He is able to do all things.

HADITH NUMBERS 602, 603, & 605

(١) ٦٠٢- وَ عَـنْ عِـيَـاضِ بْـنِ حِـمَـارٍ رَضِـيَ اللهُ عَـنْـهُ قَـالَ :
قَـالَ رَسُـولُ اللهِ صَـلَّـى اللهُ عَـلَـيْـهِ وَ سَـلَّـمَ : ((إِنَّ اللهَ أَوْحَـى
إِلَـيَّ أَنْ تَـوَاضَـعُـوا حَـتَّـى لَا يَـفْـخَـرَ أَحَـدٌ عَـلَـى أَحَـدٍ ، وَ لَا
يَـبْـغِـي أَحَـدٌ عَـلَـى أَحَـدٍ)) رَوَاهُ مُـسْـلِـمٌ .

1/602- On the authority of Iyyaad bin Himaar (*radhiallahu 'anhu*), he said, Allaah's Messenger (*sallallahu 'alayhi wa sallam*) said, "Indeed Allaah revealed to me for you to be humble and do not be boastful towards one another; nor transgress one another." Muslim collected it [26]

(٢) ٦٠٣- وَ عَـنْ أَبِـي هُـرَيْـرَةَ رَضِـيَ اللهُ عَـنْـهُ أَنَّ رَسُـولَ اللهِ
صَـلَّـى اللهُ عَـلَـيْـهِ وَ سَـلَّـمَ قَـالَ : ((مَـا نَـقَـصَـتْ صَـدَقَـةٌ مِـنْ

---

26 Muslim collected it in *Kitaabul Jannah* under the chapter "The attributes which the people of paradise are known for in the Dunya'" (2865) [64].

مَالٍ ، وَ مَا زَادَ اللهُ عَبْدًا بِعَفْوٍ إِلَّا عِزًّا ، وَ مَا تَوَاضَعَ أَحَدٌ لِلهِ إِلَّا رَفَعَهُ اللهُ)) رَوَاهُ مُسْلِمٌ .

2/603- On the authority of Abi Hurairah (*radhiallahu 'anhu*), Allaah's Messenger (*sallallahu 'alayhi wa sallam*) said, "Giving charity will not diminish wealth; Allaah will not increase a servant who pardons in anything except for honor; and no one will humble himself for Allaah except that Allaah will raise him." Muslim collected it [27]

(٤) ٦٠٥– و عَنْهُ قَالَ : إِنْ كَانَتِ الأَمَةُ مِنْ إِمَاءِ الْمَدِينَةِ لَتَأْخُذُ بِيَدِ النَّبِيِّ صَلَّى اللهُ عَلَيْهِ و سَلَّمَ فَتَنْطَلِقُ بِهِ حَيْثُ شَاءَتْ . رَوَاهُ الْبُخَارِي .

4/605- On the authority of Aboo Hurairah (*radhiallahu 'anhu*) said, "One of the female servants of Medina would take the hand of the Prophet (*sallallahu 'alayhi wa sallam*)

---

[27] Muslim collected it in *Kitaabul Birr wa Silah* under the chapter "The recommendation of pardoning and being humble" (2588).

and hurry to wherever she wished." Al-Bukhari collected it [28]

Explanation

From the ahadeeth which the author, may Allaah have mercy upon him, has cited in the book *Riyaadh As-Saaliheen* in the Chapter of Humility, is the hadith of Iyyaad bin Himaar (*radhiallahu 'anhu*) who said, "Allaah's messenger (*sallallahu 'alayhi wa sallam*) said,

إِنَّ اللهَ أَوْحَى إِلَيَّ أَنْ تَوَاضَعُوا

> **"Indeed Allaah revealed to me for you to be humble."**

Meaning, each of us should be humble toward the other, treating the other equally or honoring the other more.

From the customs of the *Salaf,* may Allaah have mercy upon them, is that each of them would treat one younger like his son, one older like his father, and one equal (in age) like his brother. Hence, he would view one older with honor and

---

[28] Al-Bukhari collected it in *Kitaabul Adab* under the chapter "Chapter on arrogance" (2088).

veneration, one younger with compassion and mercy, and one equal in age with equality. They would not transgress the rights of one another. This is among the affairs one is obliged to distinguish oneself with: to be humble to Allaah, the Mighty and Majestic and to one's Muslim brethren.

As for the disbeliever, Allaah the Sublime has ordered the believer to fight against him, be stern and harsh towards him, and deem him insignificant as much as possible. Nonetheless, if one Muslim has a treaty or covenant of protection with a disbeliever, all Muslims are obliged to fulfill that treaty or covenant of protection for as long it remains.

Afterward, the author cited the hadith of Aboo Hurairah (*radhiallahu 'anhu*), that the Prophet (*sallallahu 'alayhi wa aalihee wa sallam*) said,

مَا نَقَصَتْ صَدَقَةٌ مِنْ مَالٍ

> **"Giving charity will not diminish wealth,"**

meaning giving charity will not diminish wealth as one might assume and as Shaytan threatens. Allaah the Mighty and Majestic says,

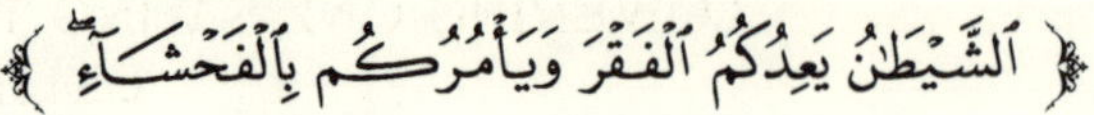

> **"*Shaytan* (Satan) threatens you with poverty and orders you to commit *fahshâ* (evil deeds, illegal sexual intercourse, sins etc.)."** [29]

The meaning of the word *fahshâ* refers to every vile thing from stinginess or other than it. So Shaytan threatens mankind with poverty and whenever he wants to give charity, Shaytan says, **"Don't give charity; this will diminish your wealth and cause you to become poor! Withhold!"** However, the Prophet (*sallallahu 'alayhi wa sallam*) informed us that giving charity will not diminish wealth.

So if one says, "How will it not diminish wealth? When one has a hundred and gives ten, he has ninety left." It should be said, "This is a diminishment related to quantity, but the increase is beyond the tangible quantity." Afterward, Allaah opens for the person the doors of provision and returns to him what he spent, as He the Sublime says,

[29] Al-Baqarah (2:268)

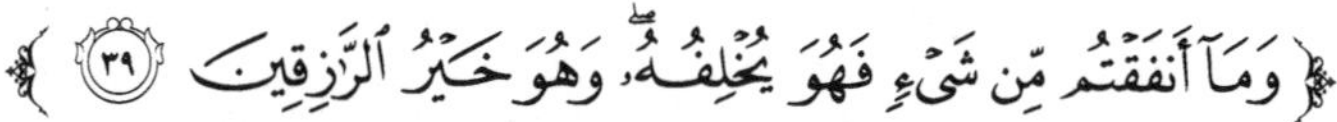

"And whatsoever you spend of anything (in Allaah's Cause), He will replace it. And He is the Best of providers." [30]

Meaning, Allaah will grant its substitute as a succession. Hence, do not assume when you give ten out of one hundred in charity, that it will diminish your wealth. Rather, it will increase it in blessings; you will be given provision from where you cannot anticipate.

The Prophet's statement,

وَ مَـا زَادَ اللهُ عَـبْـدًا بِـعَـفْـوٍ إِلَّا عِـزًّا

"Allaah will not increase a servant who pardons in anything except for honor"

refers to one who pardons the one who oppressed him. One might say, "Indeed this is a form of humiliation." Yet the Messenger (*'alayhi salaatu wa salaam*) makes clear that Allaah will not increase anyone who pardons another in anything but honor. So Allaah will honor him

[30] Saba' (34:39)

and elevate his status. And in this is an encouragement to pardon. However, pardoning is limited to that which will bring about reconciliation, based upon Allaah, the Sublime's statement,

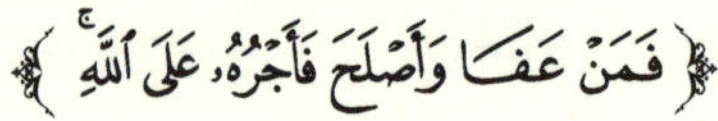

> **"But whoever forgives and makes reconciliation, his reward is due from Allaah."** [31]

So if there is no reconciliation, but corruption, one is not ordered to pardon. For example, if an evil person known for transgressing against others transgresses, should we say to the victim, "Pardon this evil person because he is evil?" Then he will transgress against others the next day and against us as well. We should say, "Have firm resolve; it is better that you punish him for his transgression." Take your right from him and do not pardon him since pardoning people who cause evil and corruption is not a reconciliation; it will not increase them except in corruption and evil.

As for when pardoning is a form of kindness and perhaps the one whom you pardon will feel

---

[31] Ash-Shura (42:40)

ashamed and will not transgress against you and others—then this is best in that case.

The Prophet (*sallallahu 'alayhi wa sallam*) then said,

وَ مَا تَوَاضَعَ أَحَدٌ لِلهِ إِلَّا رَفَعَهُ

"and no one will humble himself for Allaah except that Allaah will raise him."

This is the focus of our discussion on this hadith,

وَ مَا تَوَاضَعَ أَحَدٌ لِلهِ إِلَّا رَفَعَهُ

"and no one will humble himself for Allaah except that Allaah will raise him."

Humbling oneself for Allaah has two meanings. The first meaning is to humble oneself to Allaah's religion and not to see oneself above it; not being haughty towards it and its tenets.

The second meaning is to humble oneself to Allaah's servants seeking Allaah's face; not out of fear for them or out of hope for what they have with them; it is done for Allaah the Mighty and Majestic. Both meanings are correct and whoever humbles himself for Allaah, He will raise him in the *Dunya* as well as the Hereafter. This is something witnessed; the humble person has a lofty status, a good reputation, and is liked by the people.

Look at the humility of the Messenger (*'alayhi salaatu wa sallam*), who is the noblest of creation. One of the young female servants of Medinah would come to him and grab his hand and take him wherever she wanted so that he could assist with her needs. He did not ask, "Where are you taking me?" or say, "Go to someone else." Rather he would go with her and assist with her needs. And Allaah the Mighty and Majestic did not increase him because of that in anything but honor and high ranking (*salawatullaah wa salaamuhu 'alayhi*).

HADITH NUMBERS 604, 606, & 607

(٣) ٦٠٤ - وَ عَنْ أَنسٍ رَضِيَ اللهُ عَنْهُ أَنَّهُ مَرَّ عَلَى صِبْيَانٍ فَسَلَّمَ عَلَيْهِمْ وَ قَالَ: كَانَ النَّبِيُّ صَلَّى اللهُ عَلَيْهِ وَ سَلَّمَ يَفْعَلُهُ. مُتَّفَقٌ عَلَيْهِ.

3/604- On the authority of Anas (*radhiallahu 'anhu*) that he passed some youth and greeted them, and he said, "The Prophet (*sallallahu 'alayhi wa sallam*) used to do so." Agreed upon[32]

(٥) ٦٠٦ - وَ عَنِ الْأَسْوَدِ بْنِ يَزِيدَ رَضِيَ اللهُ عَنْهُ قَالَ: سُئِلَتْ عَائِشَةُ رَضِيَ اللهُ عَنْهَا: مَا كَانَ النَّبِيُّ صَلَّى اللهُ عَلَيْهِ وَ سَلَّمَ يَصْنَعُ فِي بَيْتِهِ؟ قَالَتْ: كَانَ يَكُونُ

---

32 Al-Bukhari collected it in *Kitaabul Isti'dhaan* under the chapter "Giving the greetings to the youth" (6247); and Muslim collected it in *Kitaabul Salaam* under the chapter "The recommendation of giving the greeting to the youth" (2168).

فِي مِهْنَةِ أَهْلِهِ - يَعْنِي : خِدْمَةِ أَهْلِهِ - فَإِذَا حَضَرَتِ الصَّلَاةُ ، خَرَجَ إِلَى الصَّلَاةِ. رَوَاهُ الْبُخَارِي .

5/606- On the authority of Al-Aswad bin Yazeed (*radhiallahu 'anhu*), he said, "Aisha (*radhiallahu 'anha*) was asked, 'What did the Prophet (*sallallahu 'alayhi wa sallam*) use to do in his home?' She replied, 'He would work for his family—meaning in service of his family—and when the time of prayer came he would leave to pray.'" Al-Bukhari collected it [33]

(٦) ٦٠٧ - وَ عَنْ أَبِي رِفَاعَةَ تَمِيمِ بْنِ أَسِيدٍ رَضِيَ اللهُ عَنْهُ قَالَ : انْتَهَيْتُ إِلَى رَسُولِ اللهِ صَلَّى اللهُ عَلَيْهِ وَ سَلَّمَ وَ هُوَ يَخْطُبُ ، فَقُلْتُ : يَا رَسُولَ اللهِ ، رَجُلٌ غَرِيبٌ جَاءَ يَسْأَلُ عَنْ دِينِهِ لَا يَدْرِي مَا دِينُهُ ؟ فَأَقْبَلَ عَلَيَّ رَسُولُ اللهِ صَلَّى اللهُ عَلَيْهِ وَ سَلَّمَ ، وَ تَرَكَ خُطْبَتَهُ حَتَّى انْتَهَى إِلَيَّ ، فَأَتَى بِكُرْسِيٍّ ، فَقَعَدَ

---

33 Al-Bukhari collected it in *Kitaabul Adhaan* under the chapter "Whoever is in service of his family and the prayer is being established..." (686).

عَلَيْهِ، وَ جَعَلَ يُعَلِّمُنِي مِمَّا عَلَّمَهُ اللهُ، ثُمَّ أَتَى

خُطْبَتَهُ، فَأَتَمَّ آخِرَهَا. رَوَاهُ مُسْلِمٌ.

6/607- On the authority of Aboo Rifaa' Tameem bin Asayad (*radhiallahu 'anhu*), he said, "I came to Allaah's messenger (*sallallahu 'alayhi wa sallam*) while he was addressing the people and I said, 'O Allaah's messenger, a stranger has come asking about his religion.' Hence Allaah's Messenger (*sallallahu 'alayhi wa sallam*) turned towards me and left his address until he came to me; so he brought a chair and sat down and began to teach me what Allaah taught him. Then he continued addressing the people and completed (his address)." Muslim collected it [34]

Explanation

Al-Haafidh An-Nawawi (*rahimahullah*) cited in *Riyaadh As-Saaliheen* narrations clarifying the Prophet's humility (*sallallahu 'alayhi wa 'aali wa*

[34] Muslim collected it in Kitaabul Jumuah under the chapter "Shortening the prayer and sermon" (876).

salaam)—that he would give the greetings to the youth when passing them in spite of the fact that they were youth below the age of discernment. In spite of that, he *(salallahu 'alayhi wa sallam)* would give salaam to them, and his companions, may Allaah be pleased with them, emulated him (in that).

On the authority of Anas *(radhiallahu 'anhu)*, he would pass by the youth and greet them in the marketplace while they were playing. He said, "Indeed the Prophet (*sallallahu 'alayhi wa sallam*) used to do so." This is from humility, good manners, cultivation, and excellence in teaching, guidance, and instruction. Whenever one habitually greets the youth, they will become accustomed to it and it will become like a natural instinct within their souls.

When one passes another he should give the greetings. Indeed we are sad that people pass elders and do not greet them, the refuge is with Allaah. Perhaps this is not done out of abandonment or hatred; however, it is due to a lack of concern and a lack of following the *Sunnah.* Ignorance and heedlessness—even if not sinful—deprives one of an abundance of good.

The *Sunnah* is to greet every Muslim one meets, and to initiate the greetings even if he is younger than oneself, because the Prophet (*sallallahu 'alayhi wa sallam*) used to initiate the greetings to whomever he met and he (*'alayhi salaatu wa salaam*) is the greatest of people in status. So whenever one initiates the greetings with another, one obtains an abundance of good, and from (that good) is emulation of the Messenger (*sallallahu 'alayhi wa sallam*).

Additionally from (that good) is that one becomes a means of spreading this *Sunnah,* which has died among many people. And it is well known that for reviving *sunan* one is rewarded twice: once for acting upon the *Sunnah* and again for reviving it. One also becomes a cause for the other to respond; and the response is a collective obligation. So one becomes a cause for the collective obligation of the other.

Because of this, initiating the greetings is more excellent than returning the greetings even though returning the greetings is obligatory and initiating it is a *Sunnah.* When the obligation is built upon this *Sunnah,* the *Sunnah* becomes more virtuous than this obligation, since the obligation is founded upon it.

Interestingly, this issue is often noted by the scholars as a curiosity, that this is a *Sunnah* which is more excellent than an obligation. This is because normally the obligation is more excellent. For example, the *Fajr* prayer, which is two units, is more excellent than its stressed supererogatory practices, which are also two units (of prayer) because the *Fajr* prayer is obligatory and the stressed supererogatory prayer is a *Sunnah.* Nonetheless, initiating the greetings is a *Sunnah* and in spite of that it becomes more excellent than returning the greetings, because the obligation to return it is built upon the *Sunnah* of initiating it.

What is significant is that we should revive the *Sunnah* of spreading the greetings. It is among the causes of love, from the completeness of faith, and a cause for entering Paradise. The Prophet (*'alayhi salaatu wa salaam*) said,

لَا تَدْخُلُونَ الْجَنَّةَ حَتَّى تُؤْمِنُوا ، وَ لَا تُؤْمِنُوا حَتَّى تَحَابُوا ، أَوْ لَا أَدُلُّكُمْ عَلَى شَيءٍ إِذَا فَعَلْتُمُوهُ تَحَابَبْتُمْ ؟ أَفْشُو السَّلَامَ بَيْنَكُمْ .

"You will not enter paradise until you believe, and none of you will believe until you love one another. Shall I not inform you a matter which if you do it

you will love one another? Spread the greetings amongst yourself." [35]

From the humility of the Prophet (*sallallahu 'alayhi wa sallam*) is that he would be in the service of his family in his home. He would milk the sheep, repair his shoes, and otherwise be serve his household. When 'Ayesha was asked what the Prophet (*sallallahu 'alayhi wa sallam*) used to do in his home, she replied, "He would work for his family," meaning he (*'alayhi salaatu wa salaam*) would be in service of them.

An example is that whenever one is in one's home, it is from the *Sunnah* to make tea for oneself, cook if one knows how, and wash that which needs to be washed. All of this is from the *Sunnah.* One is given the reward of performing a *Sunnah* of the Messenger (*'alayhi salaatu wa salaam*) and of being humble to Allaah the Mighty and Majestic. And when one's family notices one's assistance with the house work the family's love will increase, and so will one's status with the family. So within this is an abundance of benefit.

---

[35] Muslim collected it in Kitaabul Emaan under the chapter "None will enter Paradise except the believers" (54).

From the humility of the Messenger (*'alayhi salaatu wa salaam*) is that a man came to him while he was addressing the people and said, "A stranger came asking about his religion." This is a statement was used to implore compassion. A person came asking, not for money but for his religion. Hence the Prophet (*'alayhi salaatu wa salaam*) stopped his speech and went to him. A chair was brought to him and he began to teach this man because the man came out of love for knowledge of his religion in order to act upon it. Afterward, the Prophet (*'alayhi salaatu wa salaam*) completed his speech. This is from the humility and excellence of the Messenger (*'alayhi salaatu wa salaam*).

If one wonders, "Doesn't the general benefit take precedence over the specific benefit? The need of this man was exclusive and He (*sallallahu 'alayhi wa sallam*) was giving a speech to a group." We respond that if the general benefit would be lost then it is more deserving to be regarded; however, the betterment of the masses was not lost. They benefited from what the Messenger (*sallallahu 'alayhi wa sallam*) taught this stranger and general betterment is not lost.

Also, when the Messenger (*'alayhi salaatu wa salaam*) came to the stranger and taught him, an attachment of his heart to Al-Islaam was instilled within him, as well as love for the

Messenger (*sallallahu 'alayhi wa sallam*). This is from the wisdom of Allaah's Messenger (*salawatullaah wa salaamuhu 'alayhi*). May Allaah grant all of us success to what He loves and is pleased with.

HADITH NUMBERS 608, 610, & 611

(٧) ٦٠٨ –وَ عَنْ أَنَسٍ رَضِيَ اللهُ عَنْهُ أَنَّ رَسُولَ اللهِ صَلَّى اللهُ عَلَيْهِ كَانَ إِذَا أَكَلَ طَعَامًا لَعِقَ أَصَابَعَهُ الثَّلَاث ، قَالَ : ((إِذَا سَقَطَتْ لُقْمَةُ أَحَدِكُمْ ، فَلْيُمِطْ عَنْهَا الْأَذَى)) وَلْيَأْكُلْهَا ، وَ لَا يَدَعْهَا لِلشَّيْطَانِ)) وَ أَمَرَ أَنْ تُسْلَتَ الْقَصْعَةُ قَالَ : ((فَإِنَّكُمْ لَا تَدْرُ فِي أَيِّ طَعَامِكُمْ الْبَرَكَةُ)) رَوَاهُ مُسْلِمٌ

7/608- On the authority of Anas (*radhiallahu 'anhu*), the Messenger (*sallallahu 'alayhi wa sallam*) would lick his three fingers whenever he would eat food. He said that the Prophet (*sallallahu 'alayhi wa* sallam) said, "If a little piece of food falls, remove from it the harm and eat it; one shouldn't leave it for the Shaytan." He ordered that the large bowl be wiped clean (with the fingers) and he said,

"Indeed you do not know which of your food contains the blessing." Muslim collected it. [36]

(٩) ٦١٠ - وَ عَنْ أَبِي هُرَيْرَةَ رَضِيَ اللهُ عَنْهُ عَنِ النَّبِيِّ قَالَ : ((لَوْ دُعِيتُ إِلَى كُرَاعٍ أَوْ ذِرَاعٍ لَأَجَبْتُ ، وَ لَوْ أُهْدِيَ إِلَيَّ ذِرَاعٌ أَوْ كُرَاعٌ لَقَبِلْتُ)) رَوَاهُ الْبُخَارِي .

9/610- On the authority of Abi Hurairah (*radhiallahu 'anhu*), the Prophet (*sallallahu 'alayhi wa sallam*) said, "If I was invited to eat a trotter (i.e., cow or goat's foot) or a shoulder of a cow or goat I would accept the invitation; or if a trotter or shoulder was given to me as a gift I would accept it." Al-Bukhari collected it.[37]

---

[36] Muslim collected it in Kitaabul Ashribah under the chapter "the high recommendation of licking the fingers" (2034).

[37] Al-Bukhari collected it in Kitaabul Hibah under the chapter "small quantity of gifts" (2568).

(١٠) ٦١١ - وَ عَنْ أَنَسٍ رَضِيَ اللهُ عَنْهُ قَالَ : كَانَتْ نَاقَةُ رَسُولِ اللهِ صَلَّى اللهُ عَلَيْهِ الْعَضْبَاءُ لَا تُسْبَقُ ، أَوْ لَا تَكَادُ تُسْبَقُ ، فَجَاءَ أَعْرَابِيٌّ عَلَى قَعُودٍ لَهُ ، فَسَبَقَهَا ، فَشَقَّ ذَلِكَ عَلَى الْمُسْلِمِينَ حَتَّى عَرَفَهُ النَّبِيُّ صَلَّى اللهُ عَلَيْهِ وَ سَلَّم ، فَقَالَ : ((حَقٌّ عَلَى اللهِ أَنْ لَا يَرْتَفِعَ شَيءٌ مِنَ الدُّنْيَا إِلَّا وَضَعَهَ)) رَوَاهُ الْبُخَارِي

10/611- On the authority of Anas (*radhiallahu 'anhu*), he said, "The she-camel of Allaah's Messenger (*sallallahu 'alayhi wa sallam*) "Al-'Adhaba'" could not be outrun or come close to being outrun. So a Bedouin came on his camel and outran it. That was difficult for the Muslims to bear until the Prophet (*sallallahu 'alayhi wa sallam*) realized it and said, "It is the truth, binding upon Allaah, that nothing in the Dunya' will

be elevated except that it will be lowered." Al-Bukhari collected it [38]

Explanation

From these Ahadeeth which the author, may Allaah have mercy upon him, has cited within the book *Riyaadh As-Saaliheen* in the chapter on humility is the hadith of Anas bin Malik (*radhiallahu 'anhu*), that the Prophet (*sallallahu 'alayhi wa sallam*) would lick his three fingers whenever he finished his food. He would lick them until that which was left upon them from food went along with the food that he had previously eaten.

Licking the fingers after eating food has two benefits: a legislative benefit which is emulating the Prophet (*sallallahu 'alayhi wa sallam*); and a medical benefit which some doctors have noted, that the fingertips secrete a substance when licked that aids in digestion after eating.

---

[38] Al-Bukhari collected it in Kitaabul Jihaad wa Sayyir under the chapter "the Prophet's she-camel (sallallahu 'alayhi wa salaam)" (2872).

The primary concern of the believer should not be what is related to the bodily health. The primary concern of the believer is following the Messenger (*sallallahu 'alayhi wa sallam*) and emulating him since within it is the health of the heart, and anytime one adheres to the Messenger (*sallallahu 'alayhi wa sallam*), his *emaan* is strengthened.

Likewise he (*'alayhi salaatu wa salaam*) said, **"If a little piece of food falls"**— meaning on the ground or on the table spread—**"remove from it the harm and eat it; one shouldn't leave it for the Shaytan."** So if a little piece of food falls on the table spread, take it and remove that which is upon it from harm if there is something harmful upon it from dirt, splinters, or the likes, and eat it out humility for Allaah the Mighty and Majestic and out of compliance to the Prophet's order (*sallallahu 'alayhi wa sallam*). Secondly, do it also as a means of depriving the Shaytan from the food since if one leaves it Shaytan will eat it. Perhaps Shaytaan will share with the person in his eating if he neglects this issue, and when he eats without mentioning the name of Allaah Shaytaan will partake in his meal along with him.

He ordered us to wipe clean the plate or large bowl used to serve the food. Wipe it clean by passing the hand over it and licking from the fingers what was gathered up.

Additionally, this is a *Sunnah* many people are heedless of. Regretfully, even many students of knowledge, when they finish eating, may leave behind a bit of food. They do not lick the plate, in contradiction to what the Prophet (*sallallahu 'alayhi wa sallam*) ordered. Afterward the Messenger (*'alayhi salaatu wa salaam*) clarified the wisdom behind that. He said,

فَإِنَّكُمْ لَا تَدْرُ فِي أَيِّ طَعَامِكُمْ الْبَرَكَةُ

> **"Indeed you do not know in which of your food is the blessing."**

Perhaps the blessing of this food is in what you wipe from the large bowl.

Within this narration is the excellent teaching of the Messenger (*'alayhi salaatu wa salaam*) and whenever he mentioned the ruling, he mentioned the wisdom behind it. This is because mentioning the wisdom connected to the ruling contains two great benefits.

The first benefit is his clarification of the legislation's loftiness and that it is a legislation founded upon benefit. There is nothing which Allaah and His Messenger (*sallallahu 'alayhi wa sallam*) ordered except that there is a benefit in it; likewise, Allaah and His Messenger (*sallallahu 'alayhi wa sallam*) have not forbidden anything unless the benefit is nonexistent.

The second benefit is the increase in the contentment of one's soul, since one is human and perhaps has *emaan* and submission to what Allaah and His Messenger legislated; however, when the wisdom is mentioned one increases in *emaan* and certainty, and becomes zealous in performing what was ordered or abandoning what was prohibited.

Afterward the author cites the hadith of Anas bin Malik (*radhiallahu 'anhu*) regarding the story of the Bedouin who came with his young camel. The Prophet's she-camel (*sallallahu 'alayhi wa sallam*) was named "*al-'Adhaba'*"—not "*al-Qaswaa'*" on which he performed Hajj—and from the guidance of the Messenger (*'alayhi salaatu wa salaam*) was that he named his riding beasts, weapons, and the likes.

The companions (*radhiallahu 'anhum*) believed that "*al-'Adhaba'*" could not be outrun or come close to being outrun. So when the Bedouin came with his young camel and outpaced "*Al-'Adhaba,'*" it was disappointing for the companions (*radhiallahu 'anhum*). The Prophet (*sallallahu 'alayhi wa sallam*), when he realized what was in their hearts, said,

حَقٌّ عَلَى اللهِ أَنْ لَا يَرْتَفِعَ شَيْءٌ مِنَ الدُّنْيَا إِلَّا وَضَعَهُ

"It is the truth binding upon Allaah that nothing in the *Dunya* will be elevated except that it will be lowered."

Everything elevated in the *Dunya* will inevitability be lowered. If self-exaltation and arrogance accompanies this elevation then the lowering will be swifter, as a punishment. If not, it is inevitable it will return to its former, lowered state (in any case). Allaah the Blessed and Sublime says,

﴿إِنَّمَا مَثَلُ ٱلْحَيَوٰةِ ٱلدُّنْيَا كَمَآءٍ أَنزَلْنَٰهُ مِنَ ٱلسَّمَآءِ فَٱخْتَلَطَ بِهِۦ نَبَاتُ ٱلْأَرْضِ مِمَّا يَأْكُلُ ٱلنَّاسُ وَٱلْأَنْعَٰمُ﴾

"Verily the likeness of (this) worldly life is as the water (rain) which We send down from the sky, so by it arises the

intermingled produce of the earth of which men and cattle eat," [39]

meaning every type (of vegetation).

﴿ حَتَّىٰٓ إِذَآ أَخَذَتِ ٱلۡأَرۡضُ زُخۡرُفَهَا وَٱزَّيَّنَتۡ وَظَنَّ أَهۡلُهَآ أَنَّهُمۡ قَٰدِرُونَ عَلَيۡهَآ أَتَىٰهَآ أَمۡرُنَا لَيۡلًا أَوۡ نَهَارٗا فَجَعَلۡنَٰهَا حَصِيدٗا كَأَن لَّمۡ تَغۡنَ بِٱلۡأَمۡسِۚ ﴾

"... Until when the earth is clad with its adornments and is beautified, and its people think that they have all the powers of disposal over it, Our Command reaches it by night or by day and We make it like a clean-mown harvest, as if it had not flourished yesterday!" [40]

All of it will disappear; all of this beauty and all of this vegetation which mingled with every type. All of it will cease as though it never existed. Likewise, the *Dunya* in totality will vanish as though it never existed. Even the human being himself begins small and weak, then grows strong. When his strength wains he returns being weak and decrepit. Then he returns to nothingness. Hence, there is not a single thing

---

[39] Yunus (10:24)
[40] Yunus (10:24)

that is elevated on the plane of the *Dunya* except that Allaah the Mighty and Majestic will lower it.

Within the Prophet's statement (*'alayhi salaatu wa salaam*) **"in the *Dunya*"** proves that Allaah will not lower elevated affairs relating to the Hereafter. His statement, the Sublime, says,

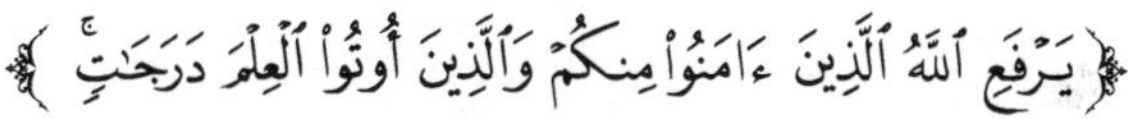

> **"Allaah will exalt in degree those of you who believe, and those who have been granted knowledge."** [41]

Allaah the Mighty and Majestic will not lower these individuals as long as they have the quality of knowledge and *emaan*—indeed it is not conceivable that Allaah will lower them. Rather, He will exalt them in mention and elevate their degree in the Hereafter, and Allaah is the One who grants success.

[41] Al-Mujadilah (58:11)

NOTES

NOTES

NOTES

Made in the USA
Middletown, DE
08 November 2024